BATTLE OF BUNKER HILL

HILL

A History from Beginning to End

Copyright © 2020 by Hourly History.

Table of Contents

Introduction

In every war, there are battles that mark a turning point, shifting the advantage to one side or the other. In the American Revolutionary War, one of those battles was the Battle of Bunker Hill. While it was a battle that the colonists ultimately lost, it was significant because it altered the way the British responded to colonial fighting forces. It was this newly developed caution on the part of the British forces that shifted the advantage to the colonists.

The battle itself took place on June 17, 1775, and although it was named for a hill in Charlestown, Massachusetts, the majority of the battle was actually fought on an adjacent hill, which later became known as Breed's Hill. The fighting occurred during the Siege of Boston which began shortly after the Battles of Lexington and Concord—the two battles officially recognized as the start of the Revolutionary War.

In order to understand the significance of the Battle of Bunker Hill, it is important to look beyond the romanticized popular history that is often told in textbooks or at patriotic gatherings. Understanding the context of the battle is key. The British Parliament had been attempting to reassert its authority over the colonists for more than a decade prior to the Siege of Boston. This greatly increased tensions between the colonists and the British Crown. The British government had attempted to raise revenue by increasing taxes, but those efforts were met with heated protests. The colonists resented their lack of representation in Parliament and demanded the same rights accorded to other British subjects. Their ongoing resistance was met with violence.

Still, even after the Battles of Lexington and Concord, there remained hope among the colonies that the disputes could be resolved without war. In fact, most sought to return to the Crown's "salutary neglect" of the colonists that had existed before the 1760s. And, the British, whose troops were the best-trained in the world at the time, were supremely confident that should war be necessary, they would easily prevail over the ragtag, unorganized militia groups formed by the colonists—that is, until the Battle of Bunker Hill. This battle effectively set the stage for how the American Revolutionary War would be fought and, ultimately, won.

Chapter One

Prelude to War

"The natural liberty of man is to be free from any superior power on earth, and not to be under the will or legislative authority of man, but only to have the law of nature for his rule."

—Samuel Adams

What brings war is a complicated set of circumstances. It is never straightforward, but instead it is the result of a tangled web of fear, misunderstanding, and competing desires. Such was the case with the American Revolutionary War. One of the first things to understand about this time period in American history is that it wasn't always as righteous or tolerant as it has come to be depicted.

The city of Boston was initially founded by Puritans who had sought to separate themselves from the Church of England because the church refused to rid itself of Catholic practices. While it is often said that they were seeking religious freedom in the New World, the intent behind the Puritans' goals is frequently misunderstood. The Puritans weren't seeking religious freedom for all; rather, they wanted the freedom to practice their own austere form of Protestantism, which often included enforcing a strict moral code. Puritans were every bit as intolerant as their enemies, and despite the fact that the Puritan traditions were effectively over by 1740, the legacy of those beliefs are believed to have been a major influence in the American Revolutionary War.

With the demise of Puritanical beliefs in New England and an increasing focus on rationalism in Europe, a religious revival, known as the Great Awakening, occurred in the 1730s and 1740s. While the purpose was to re-energize colonists' engagement with Christian beliefs, the message included a series of themes that were notably different from earlier teachings. These included the following concepts:

- Everyone is born a sinner.
- Without salvation, a person will go to hell.
- Everyone can be saved if they confess their sins to God, seek His forgiveness, and accept God's grace.
- Everyone has a direct, emotional connection to God.
- Religion should not be formalized or institutionalized; rather it should be casual and personal.

One notable opponent to these beliefs was a minister in Boston named Charles Chauncy. Chauncy supported a more traditional and formal style of religion. He was not alone in his beliefs, and the debate resulted in deep divisions among the New England colonists. Those who supported the tenets of the Great Awakening were known as "New Lights" and those who opposed were called "Old Lights."

Chauncy himself was born into an elite Puritanical merchant class family that ruled Boston. His great-grandfather, after whom he was named, was Harvard University's second president, and his father was a successful merchant. Chauncy was ordained a minister in 1727 at the First Church in Boston. It was there that he spent the remainder of his life as a pastor. As the minister of this important church, he played a role in the major events occurring at that time, including the Great Awakening, the French and Indian Wars, and the American Revolution. While Chauncy—because of his Puritanical roots—was considered a liberal by the Crown, in Boston, he and his family were part of the conservative elite class. Thus, though some of his own ideas were similar to some of the tenets of the Great Awakening—free will and spiritual equality of all men being among them—he firmly believed that people should follow the lead of the clergy since they were theological professionals.

Chauncy's main opposition to the Great Awakening pertained to the religious enthusiasm that proponents encouraged. Religious enthusiasm, among other things, specifically encouraged women to become more active in the church. At this time in American history, it was very controversial for a woman to do anything outside of her duties in the home and those to her husband. Furthermore, religious enthusiasm encouraged the development of a personal relationship with God with or without the intervention of clergy. It was these concepts that Chauncy opposed; however, he also adamantly opposed the intervention of the Church of England in the affairs of the colonies.

As the religious debate raged on between the proponents and opponents of the Great Awakening, the ideas on both sides were having an important impact on the interaction between the British Crown and the colonies. The notions of nationalism and individual rights that were a major part of the theme of the Great Awakening—and something even the Old Lights agreed with—are what many believe may have influenced the Revolutionary War.

At the same time that many colonists were pondering these new ideas, the British government began to insert itself more forcefully into the daily lives of its subjects in the colonies. The French and Indian Wars—also known as the Seven Years' War—was an expensive conflict for the Crown, and although it had brought more territories under British rule, the Crown needed new sources of revenue to pay for it. To recoup some of the costs, the Crown began to impose new taxes on the colonies. These attempts to raise revenue were met with heated protests.

The first tax that the British government imposed on the colonies was the Stamp Act of 1765. It was the first internal tax levied directly on the colonists by the Crown. The act imposed a tax on all paper documents, and part of the revenue was supposed to be used to maintain regiments of British soldiers that were keeping the peace between the colonists and Native American groups. The act also provided that violators could be tried and convicted without a jury in a vice-admiralty court.

The American colonists argued that the Stamp Act was taxation without representation. They argued that only their representative assemblies had the right to impose taxes on them. They also objected to the provision that violators could be tried without a jury. Resistance to the Stamp Act culminated with the Sons of Liberty enlisting a mob to parade through the streets of Boston with an effigy of Boston's stamp distributor, Andrew Oliver. They hanged and beheaded the effigy before ransacking Oliver's home. After this, Oliver resigned from his commission. The Stamp Act was repealed in 1766, but with the repeal, the Crown also issued a Declaratory Act that stated it had the authority to pass any legislation in the American colonies that it saw fit.

The next set of measures Parliament passed were what is known as the Townshend Acts of 1767. These taxed goods that were imported to America—specifically British china, glass, lead, paint, paper, and tea imports—and once again, the colonists saw it as an abuse of power. This time, however, the British sent troops to the colonies to enforce what they knew would be an unpopular new law. The resistance began with a boycott on British goods, but protests that included skirmishes between colonists and soldiers became more common.

On March 5, 1770, those tensions boiled over when British troops opened fire on a protesting mob, killing five American colonists. This event became known as the Boston Massacre. On that same day, the prime minister of Great Britain asked Parliament to repeal the Townshend Acts. All of the Townshend Acts except for the tax on tea were repealed in April of 1770.

The colonists never accepted that it was constitutional to impose the duty on tea that was the last remaining tax of the Townshend Acts. Their opposition to it was rekindled when the British once again imposed a tea tax on the colonies in 1773. The Tea Act of 1773 was passed as part of an effort by the Crown to bail out the floundering East India Company, which was a significant contributor to the British economy. Colonial resistance to this act culminated in the famous Boston Tea Party in December of 1773. On December 16, colonists dressed as Native Americans boarded East India Company ships and dumped all of their tea into the Boston Harbor. The Crown was furious and responded with a series of even harsher measures to control the colonial resistance to British authority. Less than two years later, the American Revolutionary War began.

The period between 1740 and 1775 was a tumultuous time in the history of colonial America. New religious ideals were dividing colonists, but one thing that united them was their opposition to increasingly strict British intervention in their lives. As the British struggled to enforce ever stricter measures, the colonists were becoming more united in their opposition to the Crown's control. That set the stage for the proverbial straw that broke the camel's back—a straw that resulted in all-out war.

Chapter Two

The Shot Heard Round the World: Lexington and Concord

"One, if by land, and two, if by sea;
And I on the opposite shore will be, Ready to ride and
spread the alarm Through every Middlesex village and
farm, For the country folk to be up and to arm."

— Henry Wadsworth Longfellow, "Paul Revere's Ride"

The Battles of Lexington and Concord are seen as the official start of the American Revolutionary War, but tensions had been building for some time between the American colonies and the British Crown. In 1773, after the British imposed a second tax on tea, the Boston Tea Party resulted in the loss of tea imports when colonists dumped all of the tea on several East India Company ships into the Boston Harbor. This infuriated King George III of Britain, who shut down the Boston Harbor in 1774 until the colonists paid for all of the tea that had been lost. It was not long after that occurred that the British Parliament declared that Massachusetts was in open rebellion.

The situation deteriorated from there, and by April 18, 1775, a physician and member of the colonial rebel group known as the Sons of Liberty, Joseph Warren, learned that the British planned to march on Concord that night. Warren dispatched two couriers to spread the news—one was Paul Revere and the other was William Dawes. They were sent on separate routes to alert residents in case one of them was captured. The rebelling colonists were told to watch the steeple of Boston's Old North Church since it was the highest point in the city. They were instructed that if one lantern was visible, it meant the British were coming by land. Two lanterns meant they were arriving by sea. Revere and Dawes were also waiting for the signal so they could spread the word. When two lanterns were set out, Revere rode through Charleston, and Dawes spread the word along the Boston Neck peninsula.

After spreading the word, Revere and Dawes met in Lexington, which is a few miles to the east of Concord. Samuel Adams and John Hancock, two revolutionary leaders, were also in Lexington, and after Revere and Dawes persuaded them to leave, they set out again where they met Samuel Prescott, a third rider who had spread the word all the way to Concord. Revere was then captured by a British patrol, and Dawes was thrown from his horse and had to walk back to Lexington. Still, the three riders had succeeded in spreading the word, and the colonial rebels— known as minutemen for their ability to be ready on a moment's notice—had already been preparing when approximately 700 British troops arrived in Lexington at dawn on April 19.

When these troops arrived in Lexington, there were some 77 militiamen on the town green. The British ordered them to throw down their arms, and as they were preparing to disperse, a shot rang out. It's not clear who fired first, but both sides started firing after that. When the smoke cleared, eight militiamen were dead, and another nine were wounded. Only one British soldier was injured. From there, the British went to Concord looking for arms. They were unaware that most of the arms had been relocated after the residents were warned the Brits were coming. The British decided to burn what few arms they found, and in doing so, the fire got a bit out of control.

By that point in time, hundreds of militiamen had gathered upon the high ground outside of Concord. They saw the fire and incorrectly thought the British were burning the whole town. They then went to Concord's North Bridge, where they met a contingent of British soldiers. This contingent fired first but then fell back as the militiamen returned fire. The first shot at the North Bridge is the one that was immortalized by poet Ralph Waldo Emerson as the "shot heard round the world."

After searching Concord for about four hours, the British were preparing to return to Boston. Meanwhile, some 2,000 minutemen had arrived in the area, and more were on their way. The fighting soon started. The minutemen began firing at the British from behind trees, houses, sheds, and stone walls. The British were unaccustomed to this kind of fighting, and after a short while, they were abandoning their weapons, equipment, and even clothing in order to retreat as fast as they could. When the British arrived in Lexington, they were met by a brigade of British soldiers—called Redcoats because of their uniforms—who had been called in as reinforcements.

Still, the colonists kept fighting, despite the British deploying flanking parties and cannon fire to stop them.

The minutemen also had reinforcements arriving, and a newly arrived contingent from Salem and Marblehead, Massachusetts reportedly had an opportunity to finish off the British troops, but their commander ordered them not to attack. That allowed the British to reach safety at Charlestown Neck, where they had naval support.

Thus ended the Battles of Lexington and Concord, but it was just the start of the war. While the colonists were not great marksmen—despite firing constantly for 18 hours, they only killed or wounded around 250 British soldiers—they had only suffered around 90 casualties, and that proved they could stand up to arguably the most powerful army in the world at the time. Though many colonists, even the leaders of the rebelling forces, still hoped that the disputes could be resolved without all-out war, the Battles of Lexington and Concord bolstered the confidence of the colonial rebels, who were now more determined than ever to resist British authority.

Chapter Three

The Siege of Boston

"I have the most animating confidence that the present noble struggle for liberty will terminate gloriously for America."

—John Hancock

After the Battles of Lexington and Concord, the British troops had retreated to Boston Harbor where they could be reinforced by sea. The colonial militiamen had surrounded the area in order to keep them contained there and block any access to the town by land. Boston at this time was much smaller, hillier, and more watery than it is today. The Back Bay and South End were both underwater. It was only later that many hills were leveled to fill in approximately 1,000 acres. Back in 1775, Boston was virtually an island, and thus, the militiamen could prevent access relatively easily. Still, the British were able to receive supplies and additional soldiers via the sea, and thus, the militiamen were not able to force them to leave the area. The stalemate would last for almost 11 months, after which the British would leave and sail to Nova Scotia.

The siege began under the leadership of William Heath, but he was superseded by General Artemas Ward on April 20, 1775. Ward formed a siege line that extended from Chelsea around the peninsulas of Boston and Charlestown to Roxbury. Boston was closed off on three sides, which left only the harbor under British control. In the days following the creation of the siege line, the colonial forces grew significantly as militias from Rhode Island, Connecticut, and New Hampshire arrived to bolster the existing regiments. Defensible positions at Roxbury were fortified as were hills in Boston proper.

In doing this, the decision was made to abandon Charlestown, which left the hills surrounding the now vacant town—Bunker Hill and Breed's Hill as well as the heights of Dorchester—entirely undefended. The militiamen and the British eventually came to an agreement that allowed traffic to move on the Boston Neck providing that no arms were carried into the town. While the superior naval resources of the British allowed them to control access to the harbor, American privateers were successful in harassing the British supply ships. That resulted in rising food prices. The subsequent shortages meant that the British troops were forced to ration food. While the American forces were able to gather information about what the British forces were doing from people fleeing the town, the British had virtually no knowledge of the activities of the rebels.

Throughout May of 1775, there were a few minor skirmishes, some of which had significant consequences. On May 10, a militia force led jointly by Benedict Arnold and Ethan Allen captured Fort Ticonderoga located near the southern end of Lake Champlain. It had many weapons but was only lightly defended. This allowed the colonial forces to recover over 180 cannons as well as other weapons and supplies. Colonial forces were also able to prevent British troops from acquiring hay for their horses. When they attempted to get some hay from Grape Island in the outer harbor, colonial forces engaged British troops and set fire to a barn on the island. That fire destroyed some 80 tons of hay. This occurred on May 21, 1775.

On May 27, another battle, known as the Battle of Chelsea Creek, occurred when British forces attempted to stop the colonial forces from removing livestock from some of the islands. During this battle, the British schooner *Diana* ran aground, and colonial forces were able to recover its weaponry. These skirmishes were taking their toll on the British forces, and that prompted the British General Thomas Gage to offer a pardon to all colonial militiamen who would lay down their arms. Notably, his offer did not extend to John Hancock or Samuel Adams, the leaders of the colonial forces. The offer was made on June 12, 1775, and rather than quelling the rebellion, it angered the members of the militia and their supporters. As a result, more people began to take up arms.

In 1774, after the Boston Tea Party, a group of colonial delegates that included George Washington, John and Samuel Adams, Patrick Henry, and John Jay had met in Philadelphia to voice their grievances to the British Crown. This was known as the First Continental Congress, and it didn't go very well. The Continental Congress agreed to meet again in May of 1775 to consider further action, but of course, by then violence had already broken out. As a result, the Second Continental Congress convened on May 10, 1775. On June 14, 1775, they voted to establish the Continental Army from the militias surrounding Boston, and they voted to appoint George Washington as the commanding general. At this point, the Continental Congress was positioning itself as the legislature for a sovereign state, and hope for a peaceful resolution to the problems with the British government began to dwindle. Those hopes would be all but dashed after the newly established Continental Army would prove its worth in the Battle of Bunker Hill.

Chapter Four

Preparing for Battle

"Let us therefore animate and encourage each other, and show the whole world that a Freeman, contending for liberty on his own ground, is superior to any slavish mercenary on earth."

—George Washington

Though the British could be reinforced by sea, it was becoming increasingly clear that they would be at a disadvantage if the militia were able to acquire enough arms to position on the hills above the town of Boston. Those arms could be used to bombard Boston and its British occupiers. As hopes for a peaceful resolution to the dispute dwindled, both sides began to make preparations.

Throughout the month of May, and on orders from General Gage, the British had been receiving reinforcements. Their troops now numbered some 6,000 men. On May 25, General Gage and three other British generals—William Howe, John Burgoyne, and Henry Clinton—began making plans to break out of the city. Their strategy was to first take the Dorchester Neck, fortify the heights there, and then march on colonial forces in Roxbury. After securing the southern flank, they would then take Charlestown, and from there, they would drive away the forces in Cambridge. They finalized this plan on June 12, and initially set the attack for June 18.

It was agreed that General Howe would lead the major assault. He would go around the left flank of the colonial forces and begin his assault from the rear. Another general, Brigadier General Robert Pigot, would lead the direct assault on the colonial redoubt (supplementary defensive fortification). Last, but not least, Major John Pitcairn would lead the British flank or reserve force.

It took a while to transport Howe's initial forces (about 1,500 men) to Moulton's Point, which was the eastern corner of the peninsula. When the forces crossed the river, Howe noticed a large number of colonial forces on Bunker Hill. He thought these were colonial reinforcements, and he sent a message to Gage requesting more troops. He stated that they needed to prepare an attack on the position for daylight on the 17th of June. While they waited, Howe sent some of the light infantry to the eastern side of the peninsula, a move which alerted the colonial forces to the British strategy. The British troops continued to wait for reinforcements and even sat down to eat while doing so.

In the predawn hours of June 17—around 4 am—the HMS *Lively* spotted the fortifications on Bunker Hill and opened fire. When General Gage awoke and learned of the situation, he ordered all 128 guns in the harbor as well as forces on Copp's Hill in Boston to fire on the colonial fortifications. This did little damage, but it temporarily halted the colonists' work on the fortifications and gave the British more time to wait for those reinforcements to arrive before initiating their first attack.

Meanwhile, the colonial forces had learned of the British planned assault on June 13, one day after the British had finalized their plans. They were told that a New Hampshire gentleman had overheard British commanders making their plans to take Dorchester and Charlestown. Upon learning this information, the Massachusetts Committee of Safety decided to erect additional defenses. General Putnam was ordered to set up defenses on Bunker Hill.

On June 16, Colonel William Prescott led some 1,200 men on the Charlestown peninsula for the purpose of setting up positions where artillery fire could be directed into the town of Boston. There was some disagreement between the leaders and their engineer about where these defenses should be located. They did do some work on Bunker Hill, but they later agreed that Breed's Hill was closer to Boston and more defensible. For that reason, they decided to build their primary redoubt there.

Prescott and his men dug a square fortification of approximately 130 feet (40 m) on one side. There, they dug ditches and built earthen walls of approximately 6 feet (1.8 m) in height. Inside the walls was a wooden platform upon which the men could stand and fire over the walls. Upon seeing the British preparations, however, Prescott called for more reinforcements. These included Joseph Warren, a leader of the Massachusetts Committee of Safety, and Seth Pomeroy, a militia leader. Both men held high ranks but chose to serve as infantry. Prescott ordered them, under the leadership of Captain Thomas Knowlton, to defend the colonial left flank.

In building a defense for the left flank, Knowlton's men constructed a dirt wall that was topped with fence rails and hay. They also dug three v-shaped trenches between the dirt wall and Prescott's location. The troops that Prescott called for as reinforcements included some 200 men from the 1st and 3rd New Hampshire regiments, which were commanded by Colonel John Stark and Colonel James Reed. Stark's men took up positions on the northern end of where Prescott's men were located, and at low tide, when a gap opened along the Mystic River, they were able to extend a fence with a stone wall to the edge of the water. Their presence filled a gap in the defense that Howe might have taken advantage of had he pressed an attack earlier rather than waiting for reinforcements.

Behind colonial lines, chaos ruled, showing the inexperience of the colonial forces. Several units that had been sent to the front lines stopped before crossing the Charlestown Neck. That area was under constant gunfire from the south. Still other units that did reach Bunker Hill were uncertain about where to go from there. General Putnam was on-site giving orders and directing affairs, but many unit commanders either outright disobeyed his orders or they didn't understand them. Under other less serious circumstances, the confusion might have seemed funny.

With both sides ready for battle, the British began their assault at 3 pm on June 17, 1775. There would be three assaults launched against colonial forces, and in the end, the British would prevail, but their victory would come at a great price.

Chapter Five

The Battle of Bunker Hill

"Don't fire until you see the whites of their eyes."

—William Prescott

Though the British assault on colonial forces around Boston had been initially planned for June 18, General Gage immediately requested reinforcements for an attack at dawn on June 17 when they saw colonial forces making preparations on Bunker Hill and Breed's Hill early in the morning. British ships fired on the colonial positions, and although they did no damage, it did stop the activity. That allowed the British to wait for reinforcements to arrive before launching their first assault. By 3 pm on June 17, those reinforcements had arrived and the British were ready to attack.

The first assault began when Brigadier General Pigot and his force, located at the south end of Charlestown village, began taking casualties from sniper fire. General Howe requested assistance in taking out the snipers. British Admiral Graves, who was the commander of the HMS *Somerset*, ordered incendiary fire into the village, which was then followed by a landing party that he ordered to set fire to the town.

Pigot's forces, along with those of Major Pitcairn, were supposed to then feint an assault on the colonial redoubt as

General Howe was leading an actual assault on the colonial left flank. Howe sent his light infantry to set up along the narrow beach in broad columns so that they could turn the far left flank of the colonial position. Howe then deployed his grenadiers in a middle position, four deep, and several hundred across. The British troops then advanced on what was actually Breed's Hill. The British were confident in their ability to defeat the American rebels—so much so that General Howe had a servant with a bottle of wine march at his side as he led his troops into battle. He didn't count on the uneven terrain and the passion of the colonists.

As the British troops advanced on the American position on Breed's Hill, in order to conserve their limited supply of ammunition, Colonel William Prescott reportedly issued the famous command, "Don't fire until you see the whites of their eyes." He told them specifically to wait until the British had closed on their position to 50 yards or less. The British, for their part, were having trouble with the seemingly open pasture they were crossing. Rocks, holes, and other hazards were hidden by the unmown hay, and fences and stone walls also slowed the troops.

When the British got close enough, the Americans opened fire, and because of the broad columns of troops, the Redcoats fell in clumps. That jumbled the British lines and made them easy targets. The Americans created more havoc by aiming at the officers, who were easily distinguished by their uniforms. The American rebels were successful at repelling the British troops at every point. When the British finally retreated, one American officer wrote that "the dead lay as thick as sheep in a fold" on the battlefield. As told by Private Peter Brown, the British "advanced towards us in order to swallow us up, but they found a Choaky mouthful of us."

The colonists, using the fence they had constructed to steady and aim their muskets, were able to inflict heavy casualties on the British troops. Additionally, they suffered relatively few casualties by using the fence as cover from incoming fire. Howe's forces had no choice but to retreat, and upon seeing what happened to them, Pigot ordered his troops to retreat as well.

The British then re-formed their ranks and tried again. This time, rather than feinting an attack, Pigot was to assault the colonial redoubt, even if Howe's forces could not help. Howe was to march against Captain Knowlton's forces who were positioned along the rail fence. The outcome of this second assault was the same as the first one—the British troops were mowed down by rebel forces. Some companies had only eight or nine men remaining by the time they again retreated.

As for the American troops, they were still in chaos. General Putnam tried to send troops to support those on Breed's Hill, but that effort was only partially successful. Some men moved toward the action as ordered, but others retreated. In one case, an entire company was in retreat, but Captain John Chester from Connecticut ordered his men to aim their muskets at them to halt the retreat. It worked, and the men returned to the battlefield.

As for the British, they were also in some disarray as the wounded soldiers lying on the battlefield continued to moan and cry out in pain. General Howe sent word to General Clinton in Boston that he wanted to try again, but he needed additional troops. Clinton had watched the first two attempts and, as a result, sent some 400 additional marines and infantrymen. He joined them to help rally the troops. He was even successful in convincing some 200 wounded men to be part of the third assault.

During the third attempt, the British again concentrated on the redoubt but changed their strategy. They formed themselves into well-spaced columns instead of a broad line, thereby reducing the target area. As the British advanced, the Americans used up their remaining ammunition, and as William Prescott wrote, the firing "went out like an old candle." The colonists began throwing rocks and swinging their muskets at the British troops, who were armed with bayonets. One British marine described the carnage that ensued, writing, "We tumbled over the dead to get at the living," and that soldiers were "stabbing some and dashing out the brains of others." This time it was the Americans who retreated, and it was during the retreat that General Joseph Warren was killed.

With the retreat of the colonial forces, the battle ended. It had lasted just two hours, but during that short time, the British lost 1,054 soldiers, almost half of those who had been involved in the battle. The Americans, on the other hand, lost just over 400 soldiers. This battle would prove to be the bloodiest of the entire Revolutionary War, and its significance cannot be underestimated. Though the British had won the battle, it was a truly pyrrhic victory—that is, the damage inflicted on the British, though they won, is tantamount to a defeat. General Howe put it more succinctly when he wrote, "The success is too dearly bought." He had lost every member of his staff and the wine bottle his servant carried with him into battle.

Chapter Six

Battle Analysis

"It is not a field of a few acres of ground, but a cause, that we are defending, and whether we defeat the enemy in one battle, or by degrees, the consequences will be the same."

—Thomas Paine

There has been significant analysis of this battle throughout the years. Many historians have noted the missteps made by both sides which, had they not occurred, could have altered the outcome of the battle. Additionally, some of the participants in the battle later wrote of mistakes or misconduct. In one notable case, American General Dearborn published an account of the battle in *Port Folio* magazine years after General Israel Putnam had died. In his article, Dearborn accused General Putnam of cowardly leadership and failing to supply reinforcements.

At the time, people were shocked by the rancor of his attack, which prompted a forceful response from Putnam's defenders, including John and Abigail Adams. Historians have noted that Dearborn's account included numerous misstatements, some of which were outright inventions, and they have also noted that when Dearborn wrote this account, he was in some trouble himself. He was relieved of a top command because of mistakes in the War of 1812, and he became the first presidential cabinet nomination to be voted down by the Senate. Thus, his account may have been an attempt at distraction from his own troubles.

As for the American missteps on which historians agree, one important problem was that General Putnam and Colonel Prescott, both of whom were leaders in the field, frequently acted independently. This had strategic implications as it was Prescott's decision to go against orders and fortify Breed's Hill rather than Bunker Hill that provided a greater provocation for the British offensive since it put colonial artillery closer to Boston. Additionally, his decision meant that the colonial forces were more at risk of being trapped since, if the British had sought to take control of Charlestown Neck, they would not have been able to properly defend against it. Fortunately for the colonial forces, the British didn't make that decision.

Another problem among the colonial forces was that, while the front lines were well managed, only some of the militias obeyed General Ward's and General Putnam's authority; others disobeyed and stayed on Bunker Hill instead of defending Breed's Hill against the third British assault. General Prescott believed that the third assault would have also been repulsed had he received troop reinforcements and supplies of ammunition in the redoubt. In fact, for their refusal to obey orders, several officers were court-martialed and subsequently dismissed from command. Still, while there were elements of disorganization among the colonial forces, they fought well against the best-trained military in the world at the time.

As for the British military missteps, one problem was that they acted slowly after spotting the colonial works on Breed's Hill. They were reportedly ready for action by 2 pm, but it wasn't until later that the *Lively* first opened fire. That gave the colonial forces time to reinforce their flanks. Additionally, Gage and Howe decided on a frontal assault rather than encircling the colonial forces by gaining control of Charlestown Neck. Furthermore, General Gage failed to use the Royal Navy to secure the narrow neck to the peninsula, a maneuver which would have cut the American forces off from the mainland and resulted in a far less costly victory for the British.

Perhaps the biggest British misstep involved their unwavering confidence that they could easily defeat the colonial forces. They felt that two regiments would be enough to defeat the rebels, and then, when General Howe did focus on the redoubt, he opted to dilute their existing forces by using a flanking maneuver against the colonial left flank. It was only during the third assault when the British feinted an attack on the colonial left flank and instead reinforced the main force that their assault finally succeeded. For his part, Gage was blinded by his desire for revenge after the Battles at Lexington and Concord, and he held fast to the belief that the untrained colonial militia would be easily overtaken. They both made the mistake of ignoring Lao Tzu's famous warning, "There is no greater danger than underestimating your opponent."

One other analysis involves the famous quote, "Don't fire until you see the whites of their eyes." It has variably been attributed to Putnam, Stark, Prescott, or Gridley, and it is also possible that one said it first and others repeated it. Regardless of who actually said it first, it is true that the troops were told to hold their fire until the British were close so as not to waste their ammunition. It is also true that this statement was not original to this context. The general-king Gustavus Adolphus of Sweden (1594-1632) had standing orders that his musketeers should "never give fire till they could see their own image in the pupil of their enemy's eye." His teachings were widely admired and repeated, including by British General James Wolfe during a battle in the Seven Years' War in 1759. The phrase or a similar version of it was also used by several other military leaders and may well have been mentioned in histories with which the colonial leaders would have been familiar.

Though in hindsight, it is easy to see where mistakes were made on both sides, it is important to remember that it is never easy to make difficult decisions during the heat of battle. When the bullets are flying and people are dying all around, it is significantly more difficult to think calmly and make the best decisions, and that is much more true for those who are inexperienced in battle. Still, despite their inexperience, the American forces did make good tactical decisions that surprised the British and repulsed their initial attacks. That is, and always will be, to their credit, even though they were finally defeated on the third assault. They lost the battle that day, but their actions gave the American forces the energy and motivation they needed to ultimately win the war. The fact that they were able to make the British pay a heavy toll for their victory would affect not only the American forces but the British as well.

The subsequent caution on the part of the British in approaching future battles would work against them, and to their enemy's advantage. The American forces had seen the reticence of some of the British leaders, and they had also noted how easy it was to identify their officers during the battle. They would use the knowledge gained at Bunker Hill to form winning strategies in many of the battles that lay ahead. As for the British, they now understood that suppressing the colonial rebellion would not work, and the war that was to come would be long, tough, and costly.

Chapter Seven

Notable Participants

"We . . . sustained the enemy's attacks with great bravery . . . and after bearing, for about 2 hours, as severe and heavy a fire as perhaps was ever known, and many having fired away all their ammunition . . . we were overpowered by numbers and obliged to leave."

—Amos Farnsworth

In every war, there are those whose efforts go unrecognized. But, on the field of battle, it is their valor that often saves the day. In the Battle of Bunker Hill, there are a number of soldiers whose contributions turned what could have been the end of the American Revolutionary War into a valuable and ultimately successful strategy that would be employed throughout the duration of that war. Among those all-too-often unrecognized heroes whose fearlessness set the example for all who would follow were the following American patriots.

Henry Dearborn was a captain in John Stark's New Hampshire Regiment. During the battle, he observed that the troops wore ordinary clothes and that there was no officer on horseback. After the war, Dearborn would accuse General Israel Putnam of failing to do his duty, and this would result in the Dearborn-Putnam controversy. He accused Putnam of, among other things, cowardice.

Dearborn would go on to fight at Valley Forge and in the Battle of Monmouth. He would later represent Massachusetts in Congress and be appointed as secretary of war under President Thomas Jefferson.

William Eustis, a physician, cared for the injured during the Battle of Bunker Hill. He would go on to fight in other campaigns in the American Revolutionary War as well as command a military hospital north of New York City. He would also be elected to the U.S. House of Representatives as a congressman from Massachusetts.

John Brooks was sent to request reinforcements for the Battle of Bunker Hill, and for that reason, he missed the battle itself, but he would continue to serve in the Siege of Boston. He would later serve in other campaigns in the Revolutionary War. He would also serve in the Battle of 1812 and was eventually elected governor of Massachusetts.

Henry Burbeck made ammunition used at Bunker Hill, and he also served as a lieutenant in the battle itself. He would go on to serve in George Washington's army as well as in the War of 1812. He would also command West Point from 1787-1789.

Thomas Knowlton was a captain serving with William Prescott. He would go on to lead Knowlton's Rangers in George Washington's Army and is considered America's first intelligence professional. He died in the Battle of Harlem Heights, but because of his bravery and moral character, the Military Intelligence Corps Association created the LTC Thomas W. Knowlton Award in 1995. The award recognizes individuals who have made significant contributions to military intelligence. Recipients must have unimpeachable integrity and the highest moral character as well as an outstanding level of professional competence.

John Stark was a colonel in the New Hampshire militia during the Battle of Bunker Hill. He would also go on to fight in other battles and would become known as the Hero of Bennington for his role in the 1777 Battle of Bennington. In that battle, he and Seth Warner were able to stop the advance of German troops and force their withdrawal.

Among the free African Americans who fought in the war was **Barzillai Lew**. Lew was a fifer and drummer as well as a soldier, and it is said that he helped keep morale high during the battle with his fife version of "There's Nothing Makes the British Run Like Yankee Doodle Dandy." He went on to fight at Fort Ticonderoga, and he was the fifer and fiddler selected to play as the British General John Burgoyne surrendered to American forces after the Siege of Fort Ticonderoga.

Salem Poor was another African American, who had purchased his own freedom and enlisted in the military. He distinguished himself at the Battle of Bunker Hill when he mortally wounded British Lieutenant Colonel James Abercrombie. His valor prompted William Prescott to cite him for heroism, calling him a brave and gallant soldier.

Another African American soldier, **Peter Salem**, also distinguished himself at the Battle of Bunker Hill by mortally wounding British marine Major General John Pitcairn. He later went on to fight at the battles of Saratoga and Stony Point.

Daniel Shays also fought at the Battle of Bunker Hill, and he later became famous for organizing an armed protest of taxes imposed in western Massachusetts. The protest was coined Shays' Rebellion.

Israel Potter was another veteran of Bunker Hill, but he became famous for his life afterward. He became a sailor in the Navy, and later a British prisoner. He escaped from the British and became a spy for France—all of this while he was trying to return to America and his farm. His life story was the basis of Herman Melville's novel *Israel Potter: His Fifty Years of Exile*.

John Paterson was in the 1st Massachusetts Regiment during the Battle of Bunker Hill. He would later serve in Shays' Rebellion, and he became a congressman from New York.

Seth Read, who had served under John Paterson at Bunker Hill, founded the towns of Geneva, New York, and Erie, Pennsylvania. He was also instrumental in getting the phrase *E pluribus unum* added to U.S. coins.

Last among the notable Americans at Bunker Hill is **George Claghorn**. He was wounded at Bunker Hill—shot in the knee—but he went on to become a master ship builder. He built the USS *Constitution*, which was also known as "Old Ironsides." Launched in 1797, it is the oldest naval vessel still commissioned and afloat in the world.

These American soldiers started their careers as part of a ragtag revolutionary force, but their gallantry resulted in them being counted among some of the most notable American war heroes.

Chapter Eight

Aftermath

"When the unhappy and deluded multitude, against whom this force will be directed, shall become sensible of their error, I shall be ready to receive the misled with tenderness and mercy."

—King George III of the United Kingdom

After the Battle of Bunker Hill was finished, each side took stock of their losses. The difference was astonishing. The British had suffered 1,054 casualties with 226 dead and 828 wounded. A disproportionate number of those casualties were officers. This would be the highest casualty count suffered by the British throughout the entire war. British General Henry Clinton wrote in his diary that "A few more such victories would have shortly put an end to British dominion in America."

Among the dead and wounded were 100 commissioned British officers, which was a high percentage of the officers the Crown had in North America. Most of General Howe's field staff were among the injured and dead. General Gage listed the following casualties in his report following the battle:

- Lieutenant colonels: 1
- Majors: 2 killed, 3 wounded
- Captains: 7 killed, 27 wounded

- Lieutenants: 9 killed, 32 wounded
- Sergeants: 15 killed, 42 wounded
- Drummers: 1 killed, 12 wounded

As for the Americans, their losses numbered approximately 450 men, with only 115 killed. Most of these losses came during the retreat. The highest-ranking officer killed was Major Andrew McClary, who was hit by cannon fire on Charlestown Neck. The most significant loss suffered by the Americans, however, was Dr. Joseph Warren. He had been appointed a major general prior to the battle, but his commission had yet to take effect when he died. At the time of the battle, he was serving as a volunteer private.

As far as prisoners of war, only 30 colonists were captured by the British. Most of these were wounded, and of the 30, 20 died while held prisoner. The colonists also lost numerous tools and five of the six cannons they had brought for the battle. Still, their performance in the battle had a significant effect on the rest of the war.

Perhaps the most significant effect of the Battle of Bunker Hill was the message it sent to both sides. The colonists gained important confidence from the battle. They had stood up to the best-trained military in the world at the time, and while they had to retreat, they had caused many more casualties than they had suffered. Despite their disorganization, they had lost relatively few men, and they had killed not just many more British soldiers, but many British officers. That gave them the necessary confidence to press on in the war and was likely a motivating factor in the writing of the Declaration of Independence a year later.

As for the British, they began to understand that defeating the colonists would not be the easy task they had originally thought it would be. They had believed they would be able to quickly dispatch with the inexperienced and disorganized Continental Army. They now knew that would not be the case. Additionally, the manner in which the Americans fought was different than anything the British had experienced before in battle. They needed to adapt to successfully fight this formidable enemy.

Chapter Nine

Political Consequences

"When in the Course of human events, it becomes necessary for one people to dissolve the political bands which have connected them with another, and to assume among the powers of the earth, the separate and equal station to which the Laws of Nature and of Nature's God entitle them, a decent respect to the opinions of mankind requires that they should declare the causes which impel them to the separation."

—Thomas Jefferson

The news that spread throughout the colonies was that the Battle of Bunker Hill was lost by the rebels, which was true. But, when George Washington heard of the loss, the casualty report gave him hope that his army could prevail in the war. One British officer wrote that "We have . . . learned one melancholy truth, which is, that the Americans, if they were equally well commanded, are full as good soldiers as ours."

The Massachusetts Committee of Safety sought to repeat the propaganda victory they had following the Battles of Lexington and Concord, and so, they commissioned a report of the battle to send to Britain. General Gage's report arrived before theirs, however, and it accurately reported the facts of the battle. This caused significant alarm in the military establishment in Britain, and they were subsequently forced to reconsider their views of the colonial military capability.

The Battle of Bunker Hill caused King George to harden his attitude toward the colonies, and it is believed that this might have been at least part of the reason why he rejected the Olive Branch Petition offered by the Continental Congress. The Olive Branch Petition had been drafted by a committee that included Benjamin Franklin, John Jay, John Rutledge, Thomas Johnson, and the primary author, John Dickinson. Dickinson wrote that the colonies did not want independence; rather their goal was more equitable trade and tax regulations. He suggested that they should be given free trade and taxes equal to those levied on the people of Britain, but if that was not possible, then there should be strict trade regulation in lieu of taxes.

John Hancock, the president of the Second Continental Congress, signed the letter on July 5 after it had been approved by representatives of 12 of the 13 colonies. It was sent to London on July 8, 1775 with hopes that the king would respond favorably by offering a counterproposal or opening negotiations. But, before he received the letter, the king had already declared the colonies in rebellion with a Proclamation of Rebellion on August 23, about a month after receiving General Gage's report of the British losses in the Battle of Bunker Hill.

The petition didn't change the king's mind, and he instead ordered that all British officers and obedient loyal subjects do their best to suppress the rebellion. These hostilities were foreseen by another member of the Continental Congress, John Adams, who had believed that war was inevitable. The hostilities that followed the king's rejection of the Olive Branch Petition only confirmed his suspicions. In fact, Adams had written a letter to a friend in which he wrote that the petition served no purpose and that the colonies should already be raising a navy and taking British officers prisoner. That letter was intercepted by British officials who sent the news of its contents to the king. Both the letter and the Olive Branch Petition reached Britain at about the same time. British officials who were advocating for a military response to Bunker Hill used Adams' letter as proof that the petition was insincere. In fact, Sir James Adolphus Oughton, when writing to Lord Dartmouth about the subject, stated that "The sooner they [the colonies] are made to Taste Distress the sooner will [Crown control] be produced, and the Effusion of Blood be put to a stop."

The hardening of the British position against the colonies also led to a hardening of what had been only weak support for rebellion, and this was particularly true among the southern colonies. There was, as a result, now more widespread support for declaring independence from Great Britain.

As for General Gage, he was dismissed from office only three days after the Crown received his report. Before he was replaced by General Howe, he wrote another report. So impressed was he with the colonial forces that he felt the need to warn the British Cabinet that in order to suppress the rebellion, "a large army must at length be employed to reduce these people," something which he argued would require that they employ Hessians—German soldiers who served in an auxiliary capacity to the British military.

Chapter Ten

Lost the Battle, Won the War

"A battle lost or won is easily described, understood, and appreciated, but the moral growth of a great nation requires reflection, as well as observation, to appreciate it."

—Frederick Douglass

By the winter of 1775-1776, it was becoming clear that reconciliation with the British was unlikely, leaving independence as the only course of action. The British Parliament, on December 22, 1775, prohibited trade with the colonies. Thomas Paine then advocated for independence in the January publication of his pamphlet *Common Sense*, which was widely distributed throughout the colonies. Colonial leaders began discussing the formation of foreign alliances, and in February of 1776, they drafted the Model Treaty, which would serve as the basis for the alliance with France in 1778. In response to the parliamentary ban on trade, the Continental Congress opened colonial ports in April of 1776, something which was a major step towards severing ties with the British.

By June of 1776, leaders were almost ready to declare independence, but they wanted to make sure they had the support of all of the colonies. On June 7, Richard Henry Lee introduced a motion to declare independence, but some members of Congress feared that some of the colonies were not quite ready to get behind a formal declaration. Though Congress did not declare independence at that time, they did form a committee to draft a declaration, and they assigned this duty to Thomas Jefferson. The committee presented the final draft on June 28, 1776, and it was approved as the Declaration of Independence on July 4, 1776.

The most important effect of the Declaration of Independence at this time was that it allowed for the United States to be recognized as an independent state by friendly foreign governments. While some foreign governments did mention the United States as an independent state, it wasn't until the 1778 Treaty of Alliance with France that the U.S. received formal recognition of independence. Many other countries would follow suit, but it wouldn't be until the 1783 Treaty of Paris, which brought an end to the Revolutionary War, that Great Britain would officially acknowledge American independence.

Between the Battle of Bunker Hill and the 1783 Treaty of Paris, there would be several other noteworthy battles. Among these are the following:

The Battle of Charleston in 1776. In this battle, the British failed to take control of this major seaport, something which forced the war to be focused in the northern colonies for the next several years.

The Battle of Saratoga in 1777. It was in this battle that the surrender of British forces encouraged France to join the conflict in open support of American forces.

The Battle of Cowpens in January of 1781. This battle stopped British advances in the south and renewed American spirits, giving them the will to initiate the campaign that would end the war.

The Battle of Yorktown in October of 1781. The surrender of British forces here was the zenith of French-American cooperation and brought an end to British military operations in America.

Though these were all notable turning points in the American Revolution, it was the Battle of Bunker Hill that first gave American forces the confidence to achieve the final goal of independence.

Conclusion

One of the reasons that the Battle of Bunker Hill is viewed as such an important battle in the American Revolutionary War is that it had a dramatic effect on the morale of not only the colonial forces but also the leaders who would later make the decision to declare independence. The battle demonstrated that a ragtag group of citizen soldiers and independent militias could come together and competently fight against a well-trained, experienced military. Had they been resoundingly defeated at Bunker Hill, the Continental Congress might have made greater efforts to reconcile with the Crown, they may have made greater concessions, and the Revolutionary War might never have been fought. But, despite some problems with disorganization and disobedience, the colonial forces fought well, and while they lost the battle, the British paid a heavy price for victory.

The increasing tensions between the British Crown and the colonies had already prompted violence at Lexington and Concord, but though those battles are recognized as the official start of the American Revolution, it took the Battle of Bunker Hill to show the leaders of the Continental Congress that the colonial forces could stand up to the British military. George Washington was so impressed by the performance of the colonial troops that only three weeks after this important battle, on July 2, 1775, he arrived in Cambridge to take over command of the Continental Army.

Not only did this battle impress American revolutionary leaders, but it also caused the British to rethink their strategies. They had been so confident that their experienced army could easily defeat these disorganized rebels that they had underestimated the passion of their enemy. That this was to their detriment became painfully obvious in the Battle of Bunker Hill. It would not be the last time they would underestimate the American forces, but it was this first time that would have the greatest impact. It gave the American forces the confidence to press on, to head into what would be the most important war of their lives—the battle for their independence. They would take the lessons learned from their defeat at Bunker Hill and forge ahead to their ultimate victory, the formation of the United States of America.

Made in the USA
Middletown, DE
12 September 2023

38399175R00027